Winter Poems

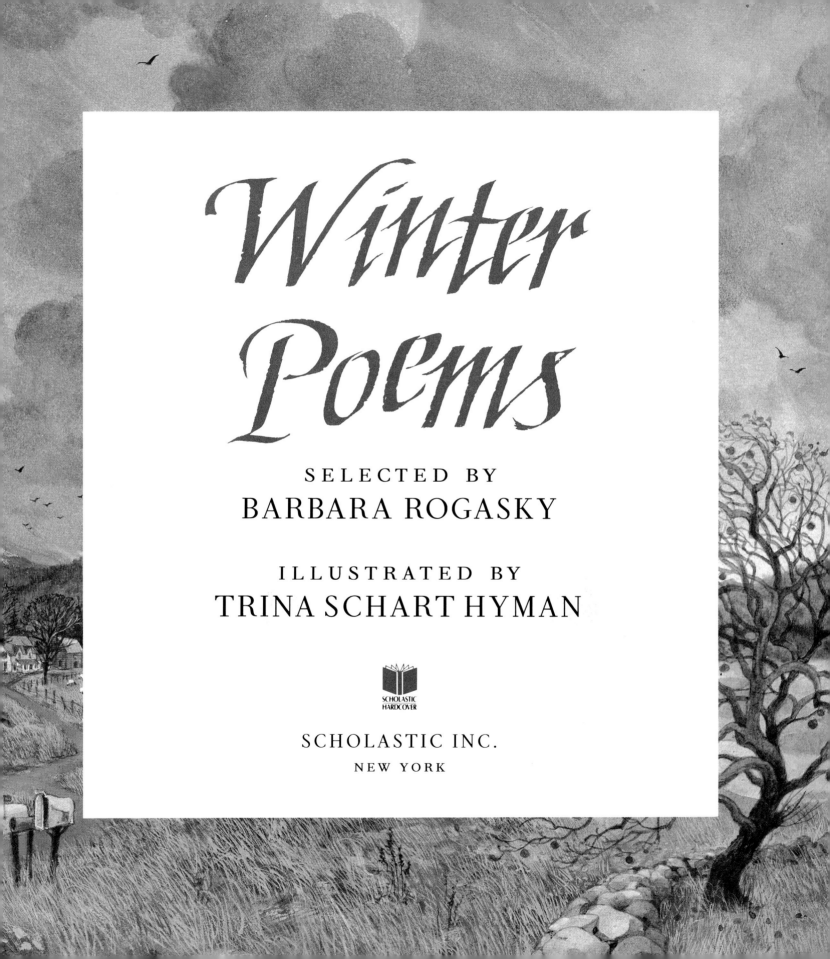

Winter Poems

SELECTED BY
BARBARA ROGASKY

ILLUSTRATED BY
TRINA SCHART HYMAN

SCHOLASTIC
HARDCOVER

SCHOLASTIC INC.
NEW YORK

TO *Oyl,*
for obvious reasons.
B.R.

FOR *my family with love,*
and for Bernard Tullar and
his faithful tractor.
T.S.H.

Compilation copyright © 1994 by Barbara Rogasky.

Illustrations copyright © 1994 by Trina Schart Hyman.

All rights reserved. Published by Scholastic Inc.
SCHOLASTIC HARDCOVER is a registered trademark of Scholastic Inc.

Library of Congress Cataloging-in-Publication Data
Winter poems / selected by Barbara Rogasky;
illustrated by Trina Schart Hyman.
p. cm.
Summary: A collection of winter poems ranging from late fall
to early spring, by such authors as Shakespeare, Edgar Allan Poe, and Wallace Stevens.
ISBN 0-590-42872-1
1. American poetry. 2. English poetry. 3. Winter—Poetry.
[1. Winter—Poetry. 2. Seasons—Poetry. 3. American poetry—
Collections. 4. English poetry—Collections.]
I. Rogasky, Barbara. II. Hyman, Trina Schart, ill.
PS595.W5W59 1994
811.008′033—dc20 91-24419 CIP
AC
12 11 10 9 8 7 6 5 4   5 6 7/9
Printed in the U.S.A.   37

First printing, October 1994

The paintings in this book were rendered in acrylics on illustration board.

Book design by Claire, Trina, and Barbara.

ABOUT THIS BOOK

Why this book? There are several reasons.

First, I love winter. In cities, cold makes the air smell better and the streets look cleaner. Snow quiets the busy racket of every day and slows things down. In the country, where I live, all the seasons are beautiful. But winter is the best. A hard walk with breath a frosty cloud is much more refreshing than a sweaty walk in the hot sun. The color and light over snow's whiteness are ever-changing and glorious.

Second, I love poetry. A poem is a kind of miracle of words. It can tell a story, flash scenes and images to the mind's eye, and use many fewer words than any other kind of writing. Try putting down in prose what "Skiing" or "Cat on a Night of Snow" is about. It'll take a lot more words than the poem does. There's music in poetry, too. Read "The Bells" or "A Winter Piece" aloud—the rhythm is there.

To find the twenty-five here, I read reams of poems. Some were written as recently as last month, others thousands of years ago. The newest in this book is by a friend of the artist from a book written for his wife—David Kherdian's "Waiting for Birds," from *The Nonny Poems*. The oldest was first printed over a thousand years ago—"Moon" appeared in a collection ordered by Emperor Daigo of Japan in A.D. 905.

There is a third reason for *Winter Poems*. As far as Trina Hyman and I knew, there was no collection of poetry about winter that did not mention Christmas or Hanukkah—or, for that matter, New Year's Eve. In other words, there was no nonsectarian book for people with different religious calendars. We decided to fill the gap, and there you have *Winter Poems*.

The illustrations are based on real things. The house is where Trina Hyman and I live. That's how the land and sky look in winter. The big dog is Jerry, the smaller one is Ben. Petey is the cat. The sheep outside are Emily, Oscar, Irwin, and Pinky. The little boy is Trina's grandson, Michou. The young woman is his mother, Trina's daughter, Katrin, and the man is Katrin's husband, Eugene. I'm "Greasy Joan" at the sink in "A Merry Note." Trina walks with the dogs and sometimes with me throughout. She holds the bucket in "A Patch of Old Snow."

We both hope that the poetry and art in *Winter Poems* bring to you as much enjoyment and delight as they have brought to each of us.

Barbara Rogasky

ACKNOWLEDGMENTS

Melville Cane. "Snow Toward Evening," from *Snow Toward Evening: Poems* by Melville Cane. Copyright © 1974 by Melville Cane. Reprinted by permission of Harcourt Brace Jovanovich, Inc.

Marchette Chute. "Skiing," from *Around and About* by Marchette Chute. Copyright 1957 by E.P. Dutton, renewed 1985 by Marchette Chute. Reprinted by permission of Mary Chute Smith.

Elizabeth Coatsworth. "Cat on a Night of Snow," by Elizabeth Coatsworth. Reprinted by permission of Catherine Beston Barnes for the author.

Emily Dickinson. "An Awful Tempest," from *The Complete Poems of Emily Dickinson.* Edited by Thomas H. Johnson, Little, Brown and Company, 1960.

Rachel Field. "Something Told the Wild Geese," from *Poems* by Rachel Field. Copyright 1934 by Macmillan Publishing Company, renewed 1962 by Arthur S. Pederson. Reprinted by permission of Macmillan Publishing Company.

Robert Frost. "A Patch of Old Snow," from *The Poetry of Robert Frost*. Edited by Edward Connery Lathem. Copyright © 1916, © 1969 by Holt, Rinehart and Winston. Copyright 1944 by Robert Frost. Reprinted by permission of Henry Holt and Company, Inc., and Jonathan Cape Ltd.

David Kherdian. "Waiting for Birds," from *The Nonny Poems* by David Kherdian. Copyright © 1974 by David Kherdian. Reprinted by permission of Macmillan Publishing Company.

Jeanne McGahey. "Oregon Winter," by Jeanne McGahey. Reprinted by permission of Jeanne McGahey.

Edna St. Vincent Millay. "The Buck in the Snow," by Edna St. Vincent Millay. From *Collected Poems*, Harper & Row. Copyright © 1928, 1955 by Edna St. Vincent Millay and Norma Millay Ellis. Reprinted by permission of Elizabeth Barnett, Literary Executor.

Lilian Moore. "Winter Dark," from *I Thought I Heard the City* by Lilian Moore. Copyright © 1969 by Lilian Moore. Reprinted by permission of Marian Reiner for the author.

Ogden Nash. "The Germ," from *Verses from 1929 On* by Ogden Nash. Copyright © 1933 by Ogden Nash. First appeared in *The Saturday Evening Post.* Reprinted by permission of Little, Brown and Company, and Curtis Brown Ltd.

Carl Sandburg. Excerpt from "Blossom Themes," in *Good Morning, America* by Carl Sandburg. Copyright 1928, renewed 1956 by Carl Sandburg. Reprinted by permission of Harcourt Brace Jovanovich, Inc.

Wallace Stevens. Excerpts from "Thirteen Ways of Looking at a Blackbird," from *The Collected Poems of Wallace Stevens.* Copyright 1923, renewed 1951 by Wallace Stevens. Reprinted by permission of Alfred A. Knopf, Inc., and Faber & Faber Ltd., London.

Sara Teasdale. "Night," from *Collected Poems* by Sara Teasdale. Copyright 1930 by Sara Teasdale Filsinger, renewed 1958 by Guaranty Trust Co. of New York. Reprinted by permission of Macmillan Publishing Company.

Richard Wright. "Laughing Boy," original title "In the Falling Snow," by Richard Wright. Copyright by Richard Wright. From *Haiku*. Edited by E. Graham Ward, Floren Harper, Houghton Mifflin Co., 1973. Reprinted by permission of John Hawkins & Associates, Inc.

Elinor Wylie. "Velvet Shoes," from *Collected Poems of Elinor Wylie.* Copyright 1921 by Alfred A. Knopf, Inc., renewed 1949 by William Rose Benet. Reprinted by permission of Alfred A. Knopf, Inc.

CONTENTS

SOMETHING TOLD
THE WILD GEESE

Something told the wild geese
 It was time to go.
Though the fields lay golden
 Something whispered, — "Snow."
Leaves were green and stirring,
 Berries, luster-glossed,
But beneath warm feathers
 Something cautioned, — "Frost."
All the sagging orchards
 Steamed with amber spice,
But each wild breast stiffened
 At remembered ice.
Something told the wild geese
 It was time to fly, —
Summer sun was on their wings,
 Winter in their cry.

    — *Rachel Field*

8

OREGON WINTER

The rains begin. This is no summer rain,
Dropping the blotches of wet on the dusty road:
This rain is slow, without thunder or hurry:
There is plenty of time — there will be months of rain,
　　Lost in the hills, the old gray farmhouses
Hump their backs against it, and smoke from their chimneys
Struggles through weighted air. The sky is sodden with water,
It sags against the hills, and the wild geese,
Wedge-flying, brush the heaviest cloud with their wings.
　　The farmers move unhurried. The wood is in,
The hay has long been in, the barn lofts piled
Up to the high windows, dripping yellow straws.
There will be plenty of time now, time that will smell of fires,
And drying leather, and catalogues, and apple cores.
　　The farmers clean their boots, and whittle, and drowse.

— Jeanne McGahey

I HEARD A BIRD SING

I heard a bird sing
In the dark of December
A magical thing
And sweet to remember:
"We are nearer to Spring
Than we were in September,"
I heard a bird sing
In the dark of December.

— *Oliver Herford*

MOON

The moon hangs up at night;
Her beams are cold and bright;
Seeing her shadow low
The water's frozen now.

—*Japanese, Anonymous*

13

A MERRY NOTE

When icicles hang by the wall,
    And Dick the shepherd blows his nail,
And Tom bears logs into the hall,
    When milk comes frozen in the pail;
When blood is nipped, and ways be foul,
Then nightly sings the staring owl,
Tu-whit, tu-whoo! — a merry note,
While greasy Joan doth keel the pot.

When all aloud the wind doth blow,
    And coughing drowns the parson's saw,
And birds sit brooding in the snow,
    And Marian's nose looks red and raw,
When roasted crabs hiss in the bowl,
Then nightly sings the staring owl,
Tu-whit, tu-whoo! — a merry note,
While greasy Joan doth keel the pot.

                 — *William Shakespeare*

SNOW TOWARD EVENING

Suddenly the sky turned gray,
The day,
Which had been bitter and chill,
Grew soft and still.
Quietly
From some invisible blossoming tree
Millions of petals cool and white
Drifted and blew,
Lifted and flew,
Fell with the falling night.

— *Melville Cane*

16

from SNOW STORM

What a night! The wind howls, hisses, and but stops
To howl more loud, while the snow volley keeps
Incessant batter at the window-pane,
Making our comforts feel as sweet again;
And in the morning, when the tempest drops,
At every cottage door mountainous heaps
Of snow lie drifted, then all entrance stops
Until the broom and the shovel gain
The path, and leave a wall on either side.

—John Clare

from SNOWBOUND

We looked upon a world unknown,
On nothing we could call our own.
Around the glistening wonder bent
The blue walls of the firmament,
No cloud above, no earth below, —
A universe of sky and snow!
The old familiar sights of ours
Took marvelous shapes; strange domes and towers
Rose up where sty or corn crib stood,
Or garden wall, or belt of wood;
A smooth white mound the brush pile showed,
A fenceless drift what once was road;
The bridle post an old man sat
With loose-flung coat and high cocked hat;
The well curb had a chinese roof;
And even the long sweep, high aloof,
In its slant splendor, seemed to tell
Of Pisa's leaning miracle.

— *John Greenleaf Whittier*

from THIRTEEN WAYS
OF LOOKING AT A BLACKBIRD

Among twenty snowy mountains,
The only moving thing
Was the eye of the blackbird.
. . .

Icicles filled the long window
With barbaric glass.
The shadow of the blackbird
Crossed it, to and fro.
. . .

It was evening all afternoon.
It was snowing,
And it was going to snow.
The blackbird sat in the cedar-limbs.

— *Wallace Stevens*

from A WINTER PIECE

                              . . . Come when the rains
Have glazed the snow and clothed the trees with ice,
While the slant sun of February pours
Into the bowers a flood of light.

. . .

                              . . . You might deem the spot
The spacious cavern of some virgin mine,
Deep in the womb of earth — where the gems grow,
And diamonds put forth radiant rods and bud
With amethyst and topaz — and the place
Lit up, most royally, with the pure beam
That dwells in them. . . .

— *William Cullen Bryant*

THE GERM

A mighty creature is the germ,
Though smaller than a pachyderm.
His customary dwelling place
Is deep within the human race.
His childish pride he often pleases
By giving people strange diseases.
Do you, my poppet, feel infirm?
You probably contain a germ.

— *Ogden Nash*

CAT ON A NIGHT OF SNOW

Cat, if you go outdoors you must walk in the snow.
You will come back with little white shoes on your feet,
little white shoes of snow that have heels of sleet.
Stay by the fire, my Cat. Lie still, do not go.
See how the flames are leaping and hissing low.
I will bring you a saucer of milk like a marguerite,
so white and so smooth, so spherical and so sweet —
stay with me, Cat. Outdoors the wild winds blow.

Outdoors, the wild winds blow, Mistress, and dark is the night,
strange voices cry in the trees, intoning strange lore,
and more than cats move, lit by our eyes' green light,
on silent feet where the meadow grasses hang hoar —
Mistress, there are portents abroad of magic and might,
and things that are yet to be done. Open the door!

— Elizabeth Coatsworth

LAUGHING BOY

In the falling snow
A laughing boy holds out his palms
Until they are white.

— *Richard Wright*

THE BUCK IN THE SNOW

White sky, over the hemlocks bowed with snow,
Saw you not at the beginning of the evening the antlered buck
    and his doe
Standing in the apple-orchard? I saw them. I saw them
    suddenly go,
Tails up, with long leaps lovely and slow,
Over the stone-wall into the wood of hemlocks bowed with snow.

Now lies he here, his wild blood scalding the snow.

How strange a thing is death, bringing to his knees, bringing
    to his antlers
The buck in the snow.
How strange a thing, — a mile away by now, it may be,
Under the heavy hemlocks that as the moments pass
Shift their loads a little, letting fall a feather of snow —
Life, looking out attentive from the eyes of the doe.

— *Edna St. Vincent Millay*

from THE BELLS

Hear the sledges with the bells —
    Silver bells!
What a world of merriment their melody foretells!
    How they tinkle, tinkle, tinkle,
      In the icy air of night!
    While the stars that oversprinkle
    All the heavens seem to twinkle
    With a crystalline delight;
    Keeping time, time, time,
    In a sort of Runic rhyme,
To the tintinnabulation that so musically wells
    From the bells, bells, bells, bells,
      Bells, bells, bells —
From the jingling and the tinkling of the bells.

                        — Edgar Allan Poe

NIGHT

Stars over snow,
    And in the west a planet
Swinging below a star —
    Look for a lovely thing and you will find it,
It is not far —
    It never will be far.

    — *Sara Teasdale*

WINTER DARK

Winter dark comes early
mixing afternoon
and night.
Soon
there's a comma of a moon,

and each street light
along the
way
puts its period
to the end of day.

Now
a neon sign
punctuates the
dark with a bright blinking
breathless
exclamation mark!

— *Lilian Moore*

31

from THE PRELUDE

           . . . All shod with steel,
We hissed along the polished ice in games. . . .
So through the darkness and the cold we flew,
And not a voice was idle; with the din,
Meanwhile, the precipices rang aloud;
The leafless trees and every icy crag
Tinkled like iron, . . .
While the stars
Eastward were sparkling clear, and in the west
The orange sky of evening died away.

                    — *William Wordsworth*

VELVET SHOES

Let us walk in the white snow
    In a soundless space;
With footsteps quiet and slow,
    At a tranquil pace,
    Under veils of white lace.

I shall go shod in silk,
    And you in wool,
White as a white cow's milk,
    More beautiful
    Than the breast of a gull.

We shall walk through the still town
    In a windless peace;
We shall step upon white down,
    Upon silver fleece,
    Upon softer than these.

We shall walk in velvet shoes:
    Wherever we go
Silence will fall like dews
    On white silence below.
    We shall walk in the snow.

— *Elinor Wylie*

SKIING

I'm very good at skiing.
    I have a kind of knack
For I can do it frontways
    And also on my back.
And when I reach the bottom
    I give a sudden flop
And dig myself in sideways
    And that's the way I stop.

— *Marchette Chute*

35

WAITING FOR BIRDS

two day old
seed-filled bird
feeder
hanging from
the porch —
having birds come
fills our home
with what is
outside
our home:
as much
a part of our lives
as the furniture
we sit in
food we eat
books we write
waiting
waiting for the birds to come

— *David Kherdian*

36

from SNOW IN THE SUBURBS

A sparrow enters the tree
Whereupon immediately
A snow-lump thrice his own slight size
Descends on him and showers his head and eyes.
And overturns him,
And near inturns him,
And lights on a nether twig, when its brush
Starts off a volley of other lodging lumps with a rush.

— *Thomas Hardy*

A PATCH OF OLD SNOW

There's a patch of old snow in a corner,
    That I should have guessed
Was a blow-away paper the rain
    Had brought to rest.

It is speckled with grime as if
    Small print overspread it,
The news of the day I've forgotten —
    If I ever read it.

      — Robert Frost

AN AWFUL TEMPEST

An awful tempest mashed the air,
The clouds were gaunt, and few;
A black, as of a spectre's cloak,
Hid heaven and earth from view.

The creatures chuckled on the roofs
And whistled in the air,
And shook their fists, and gnashed their teeth,
And swung their frenzied hair.

The morning lit, the birds arose;
The monster's faded eyes
Turned slowly to his native coast —
And peace, was paradise!

— *Emily Dickinson*

39

from BLOSSOM THEMES

Late in the winter came one day
When there was a whiff on the wind,
a suspicion, a cry not to be heard
        of perhaps blossoms, perhaps green
        grass and clean hills lifting roll-
        ing shoulders.
Does the nose get the cry of spring
        first of all? is the nose thankful
        and thrilled first of all?

— *Carl Sandburg*